ME and my WORLD

Life Online

Written by Sarah Ridley and Anne Rooney

Illustrated by Ryan Wheatcroft

W

FRANKLIN WATTS

LONDON • SYDNEY

Franklin Watts

First published in Great Britain in 2021
by The Watts Publishing Group
© The Watts Publishing Group 2021

Editors: Sarah Peutrill and Sarah Ridley
Design: Anthony Hannant (Little Red Ant)

ISBN: 978 1 4451 7338 2 (hbk)
ISBN: 978 1 4451 7343 6 (pbk)

Some of the material in this book is based on
Let's read and talk about ... Internet Safety
by Anne Rooney (Franklin Watts).

Printed in Dubai

Franklin Watts
An imprint of Hachette Children's Group
Part of The Watts Publishing Group
Carmelite House
50 Victoria Embankment
London EC4Y 0DZ
An Hachette UK Company

www.hachette.co.uk
www.franklinwatts.co.uk

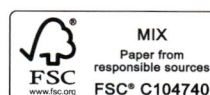

FSC
www.fsc.org
MIX
Paper from
responsible sources
FSC® C104740

The website addresses (URLs) included in this book were valid at the time of going to press. However, it is possible that contents or addresses may have changed since the publication of this book. No responsibility for any such changes can be accepted by either the author or the Publisher.

CONTENTS

WHAT CAN I DO ONLINE?

Being online means that you are connected to the Internet. The Internet offers great ways to keep in touch with friends and learn new things. But when you go online you step into another world so, just like the real world, you need to learn how to stay safe.

?

How do you and your friends use the Internet?

Things To Do Online

You can do a great deal online, such as play games, listen to music, watch films, learn new skills and find out information about almost anything. You can connect to others by making a video call, sending messages or emails, or by chatting on social networking sites.

Alex loves playing online games with his friends and uses his tablet to doodle.

Connecting to the Internet

If you have broadband at home, you can use a computer, laptop or tablet to go online. At school or in a library you can use their computers and their Internet connection. Smartphones, e-readers, games consoles, smart speakers, smart watches and some toys all connect to the Internet using Wi-Fi.

Bella uses instant messaging to chat to her friends and loves watching wildlife videos.

Being online means being connected to the global computer network called the Internet. You can connect to the Internet using Wi-Fi (without wires), cable or fibre links.

ONLINE WORLD

When you go online using the Internet, your computer links to a network of computers that stretches around the world. Most of the information that travels around the Internet comes from websites. These websites make up the World Wide Web (www).

Arminder uses her family's laptop to help with her homework. When she clicks on a website, packets of information reach her computer within seconds!

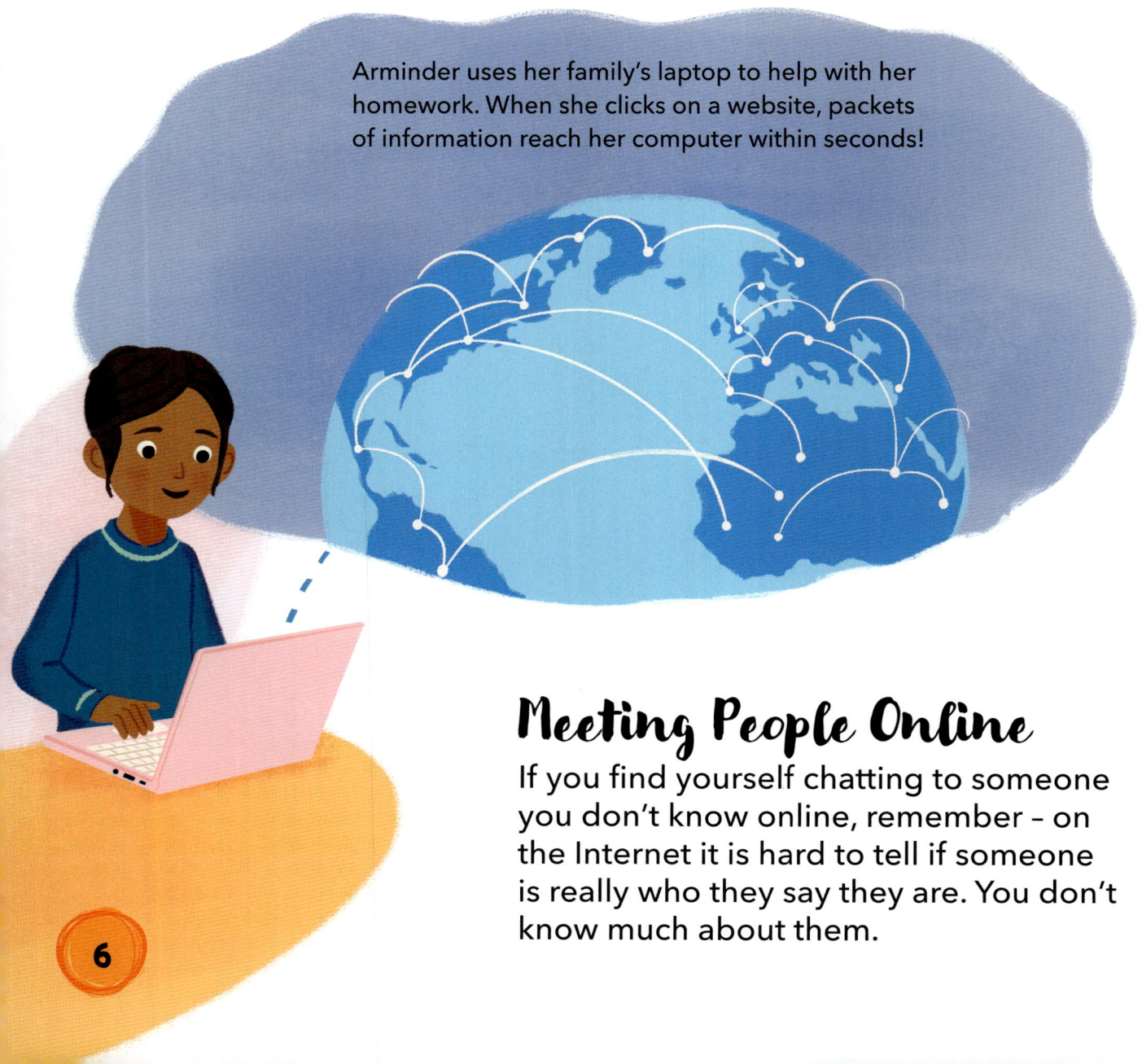

Meeting People Online

If you find yourself chatting to someone you don't know online, remember – on the Internet it is hard to tell if someone is really who they say they are. You don't know much about them.

Stranger Danger

You need to think about the online world in the same way as the real world. Just as you wouldn't walk off with someone you have just met, you must never arrange to meet up with someone you meet online. If someone does ask you to do something that makes you feel uncomfortable, tell a trusted adult.

?

What would you do if someone sent you a nasty message?

Someone may write and tell you they're your age but actually they are much older.

ONLINE SAFETY RULES

- Never give out your real name, address or contact details unless a trusted adult says it is OK (see pages 10–11 for more).

- Never arrange to meet with someone you met online.

- Never post photos of yourself or others without your trusted adult's approval.

- Don't download anything without checking with your parent or carer first.

- Treat people online with respect.

- Tell a trusted adult if anything online makes you feel uncomfortable.

USING SEARCH ENGINES

You use search engines, such as Google or Bing, to learn about what interests you. A search engine looks around the World Wide Web using web crawlers to find information and then sends each web page back to the search engine.

Learning to Search Safely

Before you start searching for information online ask a trusted adult to show you how to do so safely. There are websites about all sorts of subjects, but some may show you things that you may find upsetting. Remember: you never have to look at something you don't want to online, even if your friends say it is cool.

Ben and Izzy's dad is showing them that secure websites use https at the start of the web address.

Visit Safe Websites

Stick to websites you know about. National Geographic Kids, for example, is a website for children so there will be no unpleasant surprises there. If you are about to use a new website, ask a trusted adult to check it out first. You could use a child-friendly search engine, such as Swiggle, Kiddle or Safe Search Kids.

Fake or Free?

Just because it is written on a website does not mean that the information is correct. Learn which websites to trust, which to ignore and check information on at least three different sites and in books to compare the information.

Some websites offer a lot of free stuff, such as games, music or films. If you usually have to pay for this 'free' stuff, it may come with an unwelcome surprise, such as a virus that will mess up your device. Or it might get you into trouble as it is illegal to download films or music that are under copyright.

Jade is about to download a free game onto her mum's smartphone. Should she do this?

Make a list of your ten favourite websites and put them in your Favourites folder so that you can find them quickly. You may need to ask an adult how to do this.

YOUR ONLINE IDENTITY

Your online identity is how you show yourself online. This includes your profile on a social media account, photos and comments that you post and things that you 'like'. It is fun to create an online identity and it is important to know how to protect it.

Choose a Username

First you need to choose a username for each app or account you sign into. This is a special nickname and it is the first step towards making sure that your real name, address and other details are never revealed. Make a username quite short and use a mix of numbers and words. Don't use any part of your name or address to create your username. Ask a trusted adult to help you do this safely.

David asked his older brother to help him set up a new username for a game he downloaded.

Choose an Avatar

It is important to use a picture instead of a real photo when you are online. This is called an avatar. It can be anything you like – a sports star, cartoon character or an animal, for instance. You can change your avatar as often as you like and use different avatars on different websites.

Strong Passwords

? Why is it a bad idea to use the same password for everything?

Online passwords keep your private information private. The strongest passwords use letters and numbers. Don't use any connected to your real name or birthday. Pick something that only has meaning to you. Use different passwords for different sites and only ever share your passwords with a trusted adult.

SHARING ONLINE

It is good fun to share photos and news with friends but remember, billions of people go online every day. How will you feel if you know that strangers are looking at your private information?

Mia and Tilly only share selfies with their best friends and their family.

? Who are you happy to share photos and videos with?

Private Information

Only your family and your closest friends should know private information. It is dangerous to give this information out to strangers. It includes:

Name

Age

Date of birth

School

Address

Where you were born

Your telephone numbers

Names of your parents

Clubs you attend

Your Privacy Settings

To start, ask a parent, carer or another trusted adult to make sure that the computer, tablet or phone's privacy settings are switched on. Then each time you join an online game site, chat room or social networking site, you need to select privacy settings as well. They usually let you choose 'only my friends', 'friends of friends' or 'everyone'. It is best to allow 'only my friends' access.

Kim needs to remember to log out of websites when she leaves as she uses a shared family computer.

Locked

Safe

Risk

Keys

Websites

Photos

Secure mail

Calendar

Location

ONLINE FRIENDSHIPS

You can meet friends online in many different ways. You can share news, jokes, photos and weblinks on social networking sites or play online games. Some games have a 'chat' window, which you can use to chat and text.

You can be whoever you want to be online, but remember that other people can do the same. They might present a view of themselves that is false.

Same Difference

Although you need to learn some new skills to be a good friend online, in many ways it is not so different. So, be kind, treat people fairly, show you care about them, respect your friends' differences, be there for friends when they are feeling down, make them giggle when you tell them something funny and share happy moments with them.

Darcy is fed up of seeing Holly's holiday photos. It just makes her feel jealous and sad that her family are not going on holiday this year.

Posting Photos

Learn to be a good online friend: think before you post. Once words or photos have been posted you can't get them back. If you are about to post a photo of your friends, ask yourself: will it upset them, or will it make them laugh? Does the photo give away too much private information such as their name, address or the school they attend?

?

What would you do if someone you don't know invited you to be their friend online?

David will only send this photo to Charis because it shows which swimming club Charis belongs to.

CHATTING ONLINE

Tapping out text conversations is a great way of keeping in touch. With instant messaging applications (apps) you can chat anywhere. You can also have text conversations with kids from all over the world in online chat rooms.

Vinnie speaks to his grandfather in India using video calls. It is almost as good as having him in the room.

Video Chat

If your computer or tablet has a webcam, you can use video chat to keep in touch. Only ever use video chat with people you know really well. Always make sure your location settings are turned off on whichever device you are using.

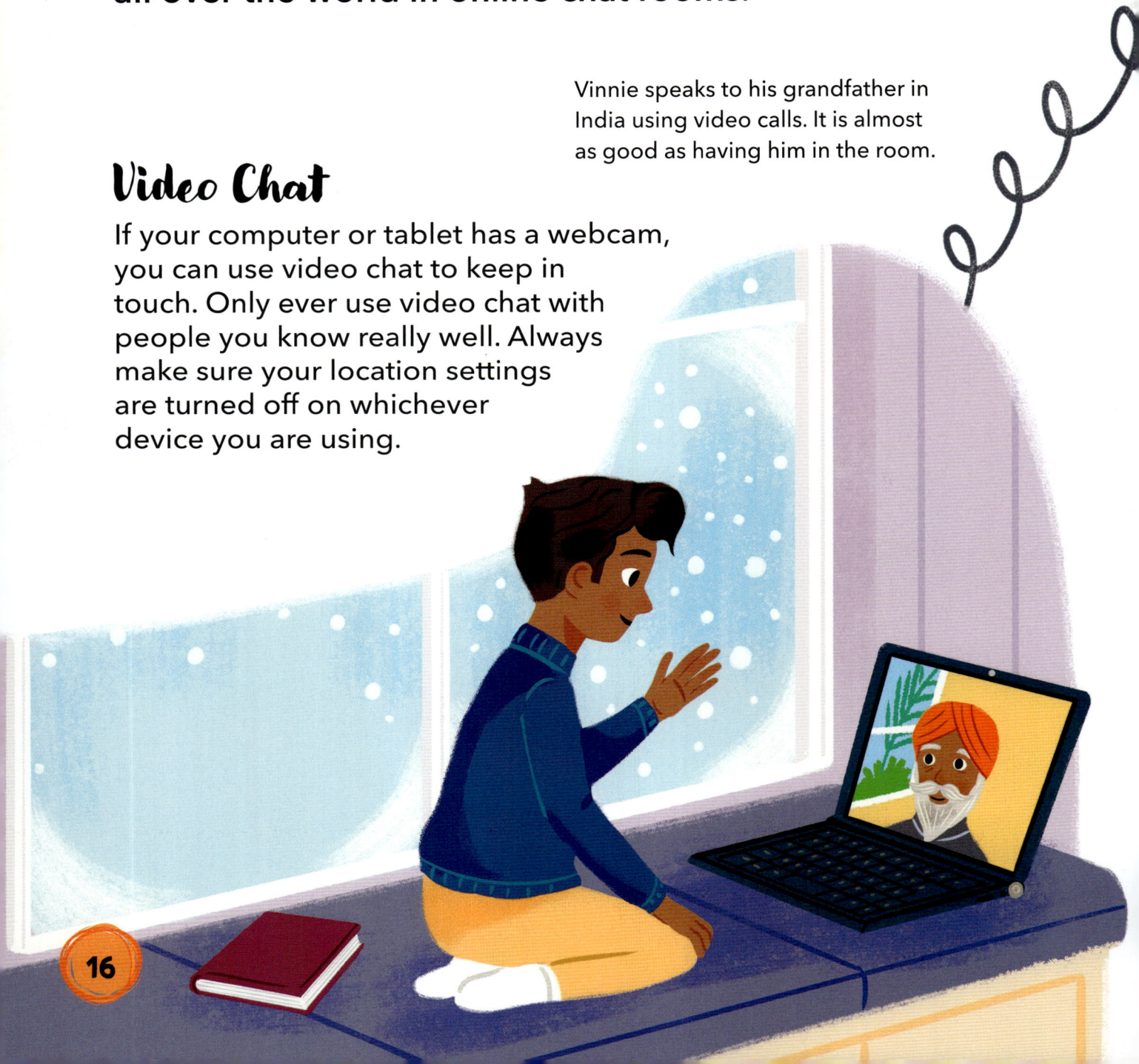

Vinnie's grandfather lives in India. Video calls help them both stay in touch.

Chat Room Strangers

In a chat room, everyone is a stranger. Because everyone uses an avatar, which protects their privacy, you don't know who they are in real life. Some people in chat rooms are pretending to be children. If someone seems overly keen to become online friends with you and it is making you feel uncomfortable, tell a trusted adult and the chat-room moderator.

Moderators

Moderators are people who keep an eye on chat sites. If you want to use chat rooms, game sites or social networking sites, make sure they are spaces for children and that they have a moderator.

PLAYING GAMES ONLINE

Lots of people enjoy playing games online. They can be fun and some of them teach you things, such as Minecraft. You can play a single player game on a phone or tablet or play with others on your games console or computer. When you are playing a multiplayer game, you can chat to the other gamers.

Strike a Balance

You probably talk about the games you play online with your friends at school, or play games with them when you have them over to your house. However, it is easy to forget how long you have been playing a game. That can leave you with little time for other interests, family life or spending time with friends in real life.

Eddie sets an alarm to remind him when to stop his online gaming session. He has lots of other interests.

Free or Not?

Some online games are free to use and download. Others cost money. Always ask your parents or carers before you set up an account where you have to use a debit card to pay for access to a game. Always ask an adult before you click 'buy' or 'purchase'.

? How do you keep your information private on an online game?

Gemma's mum showed her how to block someone on her mini tablet.

It's Just a Game

If someone sends you a mean message, such as calling you a loser, never reply to the message. Ask your trusted adult to show you how to block people. If you don't know the person in real life, just chat about the game and remember to take breaks. It is possible on some sites to set privacy settings so that you only play with friends you know in real life.

Some children become addicted to online gaming. It is all they can think about and they sneak back online when their parents think they are asleep. This makes them tired, affects their schoolwork and stops them from thinking about anything else.

USING EMAIL

Email is a good way to keep in touch with family and friends. Sometimes though, you get an email from someone you don't know. When that happens, you need to take care.

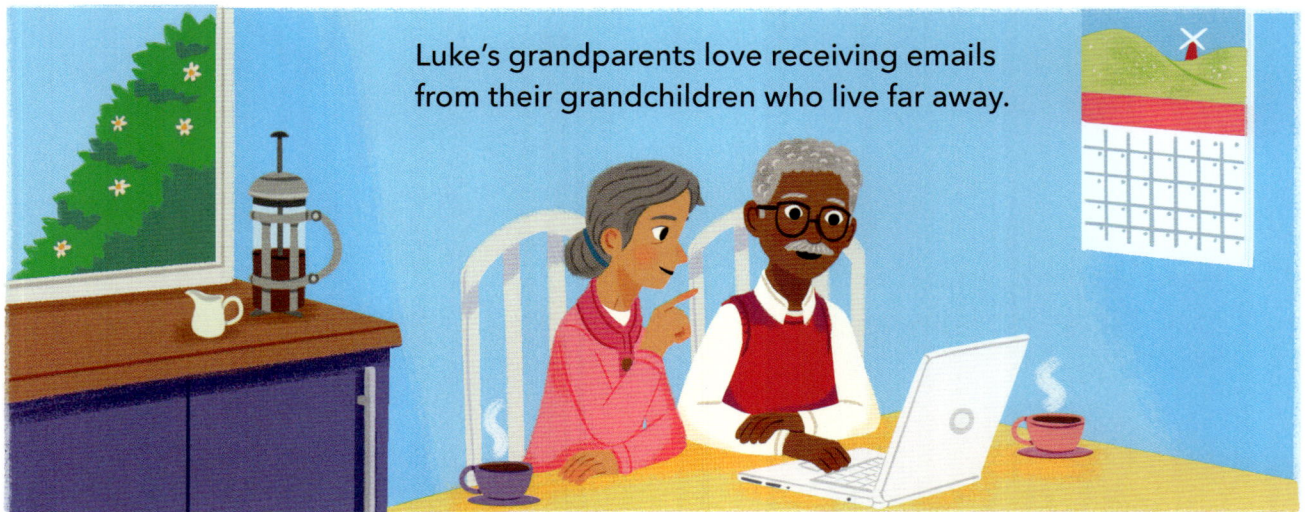

Luke's grandparents love receiving emails from their grandchildren who live far away.

Spam Emails

Unknown and unwanted emails are called spam. Always check a new email carefully before opening it. It may try to get you to buy something or offer a free gift. It is best to delete spam without opening it by clicking the 'junk' or 'spam' button.

Fake Emails

Some people or organisations send out fake emails to millions of people's email addresses hoping that someone will reply. If they do reply, the sender knows that the email address is real. Then they bombard that person with spam.

Viruses and Malware

Emails are a quick way to send computer files or photos to people as attachments. The trouble is that bad people also send viruses and malware as email attachments. Sometimes these attachments look like something you would like so BEWARE. Viruses and malware are software designed to harm your computer or device. Never open these emails and instead delete them straight away.

Dylan opened a spam email and accidentally downloaded a virus. Now his computer will have to go to an expert to be cleaned up.

VIRUS ALERT!

?

Who would you be happy to send emails to and get emails from?

Take care what you write about other people in an email. Once you have sent it, you can't get it back.

USING A MOBILE PHONE

You may not own a mobile phone but you probably will one day. Mobile phones allow us to talk, text, take photos, make short videos and connect to the Internet from anywhere. Once online, you can use instant messaging apps to contact friends and upload photos and videos to social media accounts.

Passcode Protect

People take their mobile phones everywhere, so it is quite easy to lose them or leave them behind. If you have set up a passcode, no one will be able to get into your phone to use it or steal any personal information on it. A passcode is like a password but it is made up of numbers.

Harry's mum is always taking photos of him and posting them online. Harry wishes she would ask his permission as sometimes it is embarrassing!

Phone Bills

Phone use is not free. The bill payer in your family will have an arrangement with a mobile phone network. This will usually allow the phone user to make a certain number of calls and texts and allow them to go online for a set amount of time. Check with the bill payer before you use the Internet on a smartphone or you could land them with a big bill.

? *What should you share on a mobile phone?*

Always On

You will have noticed that some adults are always on their phones. This is not a good habit as it is tiring, it stops them from doing things properly, they don't have time for family life or friends, it uses up all their free time and it can affect their sleep. The same is true for you! Why not set some good family rules about phone use?

FAMILY PHONE RULES

- No phones at the dining table.
- Switch off phones two hours before bedtime.
- Set a limit for time spent on the phone.
- Agree which websites and games you can go on.
- Ask permission before posting photos of each other.
- Only share family phone numbers within the family.

23

CYBER BULLYING

Someone who says nasty things and spreads lies about others online is a cyber bully. It can be someone you know or a stranger. The person sends you messages that upset or frighten you, posts nasty comments or makes fun of you over and over again.

Why?

Cyber bullies are often going through bad times themselves, or they may bully to get attention. They hide behind the computer and say things that they would probably never say face-to-face. Cyber bullying can happen to anyone. It is not your fault and the best thing to do is to take action to try to stop it.

? Does your school have an anti-bullying charter? Could you help set one up?

Beat Bullying

- Never reply to a bully's messages.

- Tell a trusted adult what is happening and ask for their help.

- Take a screenshot of every nasty message as proof. (Ask an adult to show you how to do this.)

- Only answer your phone if it is coming from a number you recognise.

- Block and report a bully if the website allows this.

- Tell your close friends what is happening.

Ben has no idea who is sending him horrible messages on his phone. He is going to show them to his mum.

Bystanders

You can become a bystander if you watch someone being picked on in real life or online and do nothing to help. You may be worried about getting involved. You may even 'like' the nasty things they write about people. If you have become a bystander, tell an adult what's going on, listen to the person who is being bullied and offer your support.

WHAT HAPPENS WHEN THINGS GO WRONG ONLINE?

The Internet is amazing. You can find out so much information, learn your favourite songs or stay in touch with friends and family. However, even if you are careful, sometimes things go wrong. If something bad happens, always tell a trusted adult.

Pippa uses the Internet to show her how to grow vegetables in pots. She stays away from chat rooms because someone was unkind to her there.

What If Someone is Nasty Online?

If someone writes a nasty comment about your photo, is unkind in a chat room or sends you a horrible message, don't respond or reply. Block them, stop being their online friend and tell a trusted adult. If you only allow your real friends to access private spaces, such as your social media wall, you are much less likely to run into trouble.

How to Report Bad Things

You can use the 'report abuse' button on websites to report someone who says something nasty or upsetting. Show the upsetting comment or picture to a trusted adult before deleting it and asking for their help.

Look After Your Digital Footprint

Every time you go online you leave a trail of information called your digital footprint. It shows others what you have searched for and what you have done there. Once you post a photo or a comment online, it is there forever. If you would not show a photo or comment to your mum, don't post it!

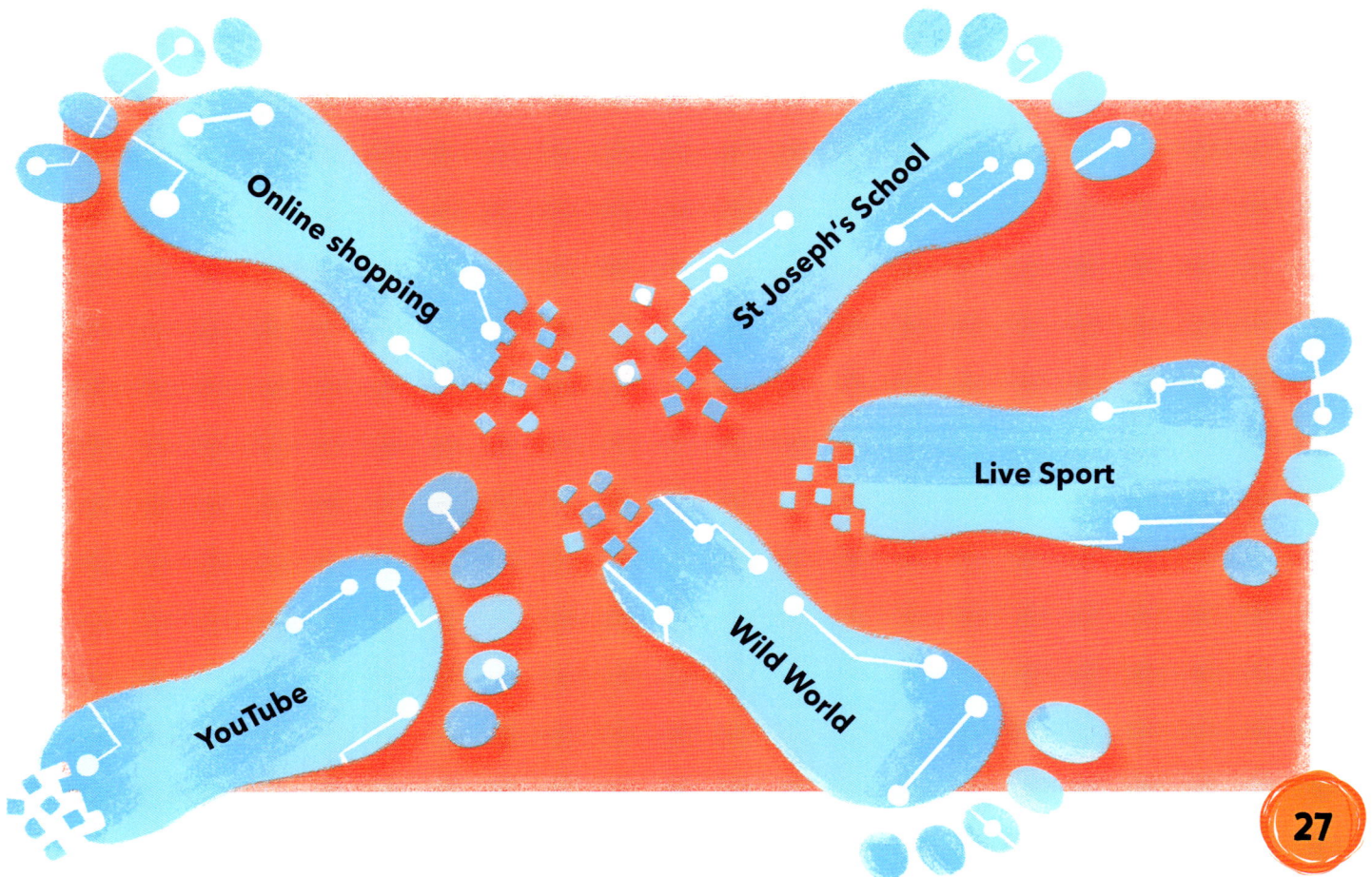

Online shopping

St Joseph's School

Live Sport

YouTube

Wild World

THINGS TO TALK ABOUT AND DO

Before You Begin

Talk about how you use the Internet. What do you like doing online? What have you learnt from the book that will help you to stay safe online?

Think and Talk

Be Aware

Many websites and games for children are businesses that need to make money. They collect lots of information about you and sell this to advertisers who pay them to show you adverts. Never click on pop-up adverts or messages. They might be adverts trying to get your attention to buy something. What else might happen if you click on pop-ups or links in emails?

Write

Wonderful World Wide Web

Do some online research to write a short biography, or draw a comic-strip story, about Tim Berners-Lee. He invented the World Wide Web (www).

Where was he born?

What did he like playing with when he was a child?

What did he study at university?

When did he invent the World Wide Web?

How did it work?

Create

Art Online

You can see wonderful art by exploring the websites of art galleries and museums. Let them inspire you to make or paint something yourself. There are also some fun online paint programs such as Tate Paint at: **https://www.tate.org.uk/kids/games-quizzes/tate-paint**

Learn to Code

Learn how to code in Scratch, a free programming language and online community where you can create stories, games and animations. Here is the website: **https://scratch.mit.edu/about**

29

GLOSSARY

addicted A strong habit that makes it difficult to stop doing something.

app Short for application program. An app allows you to do things online, such as play a game or type out a story you have written.

attachment A document you send someone attached to an email.

block Stop someone sending messages to you.

broadband A way of connecting to the Internet.

chat A conversation carried out in text by typing in a message window on a computer or other device.

copyright Owning something, such as a song or a video game, and being the only person who is allowed to copy it without asking permission from the copyright owner.

cyber bullying Using mobile phones, computers and other devices to send messages, texts or comments in order to upset somebody.

download To copy a file from the Internet onto your computer or device.

https (Hypertext Transfer Protocol Secure) It allows information to be safely sent around the World Wide Web using the Internet.

Internet The huge network of computers connected to each other around the world that can share information.

log out/log off Close the connection between your device and an online account or application.

malware Similar to a computer virus, malware harms your computer or other device, slows it down and can steal private information from your computer.

moderator An adult whose job it is to make sure that a chat site is safe for children to use.

post Putting a message online.

privacy settings The part of a social media website that allows you to control who sees your comments, text or photos on that website.

respect Treating people kindly and politely, just as you'd like to be treated yourself.

selfie A photo you take of yourself, usually with a mobile phone.

social networking site An online space where people can connect to each other by messaging or posting images and videos.

software The programmes (or instructions) that tell a computer what to do.

upload To add videos, photos or other data onto social networking sites.

video call An Internet connection that allows people to chat face-to-face through their computer screens.

virus On computers, a piece of computer code designed to damage a computer or other device.

webcam A video camera that connects to your computer or other device. It records what it sees and this can immediately be seen on another computer or device.

website A web page or a group of web pages.

www (World Wide Web) A collection of web pages on the Internet.

TRUSTED ADULTS

Throughout this book, the author advises you to talk to a trusted adult if you are upset, afraid or confused. A trusted adult is someone you are happy to be around and who listens to what you say, or someone who has helped you before. It can be many people including your teacher, a teaching assistant, a nurse, your parents, an older sibling or your grandparents. Not all adults are trusted adults.

FURTHER INFORMATION

WEBSITES IN THE UK

BBC: Eight top tips for staying safe online at: **www.bbc.co.uk/cbbc/findoutmore/ help-me-out-staying-safe-online**

Childnet International: Get SMART with Childnet International's top tips for how to stay safe online at: **www.childnet.com/ young-people/primary/get-smart**

Internet Matters: This organisation has many resources to help children stay safe online at: **www.internetmatters. org/schools-esafety/primary**

NSPCC: Advice to families about how to keep children safe online at: **www.nspcc. org.uk/keeping-children-safe/online- safety/internet-connected-devices**

Safer Internet Day: Each year in February, people all around the world mark Safer Internet Day. Find out more about it here:

**www.saferinternetday.org
www.saferinternet.org.uk**

WEBSITES IN AUSTRALIA

Australian Government: Tips for staying safe online and details about Safer Internet Day at:

www.esafety.gov.au/kids/I-want- help-with/being-safe-online

www.esafety.gov.au/safer-internet-day

kidshelpline: This charity has online resources about cyberbullying, staying safe online, online gaming and much more at: **kidshelpline.com.au/kids/issues**

Save the Children: Information for parents on how to keep their children safe online at: **www.savethechildren.org.au/our- stories/children-s-online-safety**

INDEX